W9-DFP-113

WITHDRAWN

Simply Science
WEATHER
Discover Science Through Facts and Fun

By Felicia Law and Steve Way

Science and curriculum consultant:

Debra Voege, M.A., science curriculum resource teacher

Gareth Stevens
Publishing

Please visit our web site at www.garethstevens.com.
For a free catalog describing our list of high-quality books, call 1-800-542-2595 (USA) or 1-800-387-3178 (Canada). Our fax: 1-877-542-2596

Library of Congress Cataloging-in-Publication Data

Law, Felicia.
    Weather/by Felicia Law.
        p. cm.—(Simply Science)
    Includes bibliographical references and index.
    ISBN-10: 0-8368-9233-X   ISBN-13: 978-0-8368-9233-8 (lib. bdg.)
    1. Weather—Juvenile literature. 2. Climatology—Juvenile literature. I. Title.
QC981.3.L388   2009
551.5—dc22
                              2008012424

This North American edition first published in 2009 by
Gareth Stevens Publishing
A Weekly Reader® Company
1 Reader's Digest Road
Pleasantville, NY 10570-7000 USA

This edition copyright © 2009 by Gareth Stevens, Inc. Original edition copyright © 2007 by Diverta Publishing Ltd., First published in Great Britain by Diverta Publishing Ltd., London, UK.

Gareth Stevens Senior Managing Editor: Lisa M. Herrington
Gareth Stevens Creative Director: Lisa Donovan
Gareth Stevens Designer: Keith Plechaty
Gareth Stevens Associate Editor: Amanda Hudson
Special thanks to Mark Sachner

Photo Credits: Cover (tc) Jakob Metzger/Shutterstock Inc., (bl) Jhaz Photography/Shutterstock Inc.; p. 4-5 Daniel Leclair/Corbis; p. 6 Nikola Bilic/Shutterstock Inc.; p. 8 Pot of Grass Productions/Shutterstock Inc.; p. 9 Jim Reed/Corbis; p. 10 (cl) Jim Reed/Science Photo Library, (c) Andrey Plis/Shutterstock Inc., (cr) David Lewis/Shutterstock Inc.; p. 11 Lars Christensen/Shutterstock Inc.; p. 13 (tl) Jostein Hauge/Shutterstock Inc., (r) Bateleur/Shutterstock Inc. p. 14 Jens Mayer/Shutterstock Inc. p. 14-15 Mihaicalin/Shutterstock Inc.; p. 15 Mark Bond/Shutterstock Inc.; p. 16-17 Jan Martin Will/Shutterstock Inc.; p. 17 Bernhard Edmaier/Science Photo Library; p. 18 Darla Hallmark/Shutterstock Inc.; p. 20 Jhaz Photography/Shutterstock Inc.; p. 22 (cl) NASA/JPL, (tr) NASA/Dryden Flight Research Center; p. 22-23 NASA; p. 24 Jozef Sedmak/Shutterstock Inc.; p. 25 Jakob Metzger/Shutterstock Inc.; p. 26 (bl) Hugo Maes/Shutterstock Inc., (br) Chee-Onn Leong/Shutterstock Inc.; p. 27 (tr) Zastavkin/Shutterstock Inc., (cr) Olga Shelego/Shutterstock Inc., (bl) Hinrich Baesemann/Corbis, (br) Pichugin Dmitry/Shutterstock Inc.

Illustrations: Steve Boulter and Xact Studio

Diagrams: Ralph Pitchford

Every effort has been made to trace the copyright holders for the photos used in this book, and the publisher apologizes in advance for any unintentional omissions. We would be pleased to insert the appropriate acknowledgements in any subsequent edition of this publication.

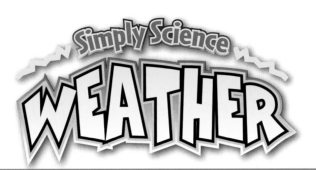

CONTENTS

What Is Weather?

What's the weather like today? Is the rain pouring so hard that you can't play outdoors? Is it so hot that you need a cool shower? Or is it so cold that you're wearing two layers of sweaters? You can't get away from the weather. It changes all the time, and it forces you to change with it!

Weather is about lots of things. It's about the temperature of a place—how hot or cold it is. Weather is about the air and whether the air is moving up or down in the atmosphere.

Weather is about the kind of wind that's blowing, and it's about measuring how much rain is falling—or not falling.

Weather is all about what is happening in the atmosphere that surrounds our Earth.

Weather can be:

rainy and damp . . .

dry . . .

hot . . .

icy cold . . .

stormy . . .

. . . or calm

4

Lighthouses are built to keep standing in the worst weather!

When the Wind Blows

Wind is the movement of air surrounding Earth. There is almost always some wind, even if it's very light. Winds usually begin when air moves from an area of high pressure to one of low pressure.

Measuring the Atmospheric Pressure

A **barometer** is an instrument that is used to measure pressure in the atmosphere. An aneroid barometer has a dial marked in units of pressure. As the pressure changes, a needle moves on the dial. This shows how much the pressure is increasing or decreasing.

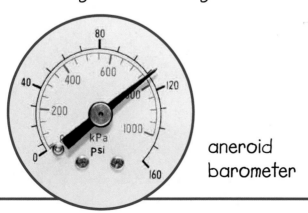

aneroid barometer

High and Low

Scientists measure the weight of the air that is pressing down on Earth. This measurement is called **atmospheric pressure**. The lower the ground, the more air is pressing down on it. So pressure is higher in a valley and lower on top of a mountain.

In a **high pressure** area, the atmospheric pressure is greater. High pressure usually means clear, dry weather.

In a **low pressure** area, such as on top of a mountain, the low atmospheric pressure may mean cooler, wet weather.

World Winds

Polar winds are cold. They blow out of the Arctic and Antarctic.

Trade winds blow around the tropics toward the **equator**.

Monsoons change direction with the seasons. Summer monsoons are mainly westerly and bring lots of rain. Winter monsoons tend to be easterly and cause **drought**.

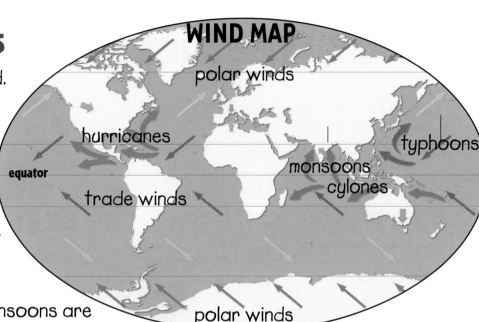

WIND MAP

polar winds

hurricanes

equator

trade winds

monsoons

cylones

typhoons

polar winds

Many Winds Have Special Names:

The **mistral** and **sirocco** blow around Mediterranean countries.

The **brickfielder** is a wind from the desert of southern Australia.

A **chubasco** is a violent squall with thunder and lightning, during the rainy season along the west coast of Central America.

The **elephanta** is a strong southerly wind that blows on the Malabar coast of India.

Sharki is a southeasterly wind that sometimes blows in the Persian Gulf.

A **willy-willy** is a tropical cyclone in Australia.

The **chinook** blows down the eastern slopes of the Rocky Mountains.

Which Way?

You can always tell which way the wind is blowing by wetting your finger and holding it up. Your finger will feel colder on the part that the wind is blowing on.

Windy Weather

The strength of the wind is measured by scientists using the Beaufort scale. This scale goes from 0 to 12. It measures the effect of the wind on land.

Hang onto your hat!

Anemometer and Weather Vane

An **anemometer** is an instrument that measures the speed of the wind. The wind turns small cups that are attached to a rod. The harder the wind is blowing, the faster the cups turn. A weather vane shows which direction the wind is blowing.

The Beaufort Scale

0 Calm
Smoke rises straight up.

1 Light air
Only the lightest things are stirred.

2 Light wind
Breeze felt on face; leaves rustle.

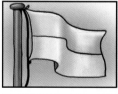

3 Gentle breeze
Leaves and small twigs in motion; light flag will move.

4 Moderate breeze
Raises dust and loose paper; small branches are moved.

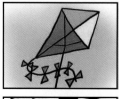

5 Fresh breeze
Leaves on trees begin to sway; good weather for flying kites!

6 Strong breeze
Large branches in motion; whistling heard in phone wires.

Hurricanes, Cyclones, and Typhoons

A hurricane has strong winds and blows in a circular pattern. There is an area of calm at the center of a hurricane called the eye. The wind swirls around the eye. Hurricanes bring heavy rain and thunderstorms.

A cyclone is a hurricane that blows in from the Indian or Pacific oceans. A hurricane blowing in from the northern Pacific is called a typhoon. Hurricanes destroy property. They can raise the sea level 20 feet (6 meters) higher than normal.

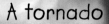

A tornado

7 Near gale
Whole trees in motion; difficult to walk against the wind.

8 Gale
Twigs break off trees; stops people from walking forward.

9 Strong gale
Slight structural damage occurs (such as roof damage).

10 Severe gale
Seldom experienced inland; trees uprooted; structural damage occurs.

11 Violent storm
Storm accompanied by widespread damage.

12 Hurricane
Widespread damage can occur; flooding near the coast.

Tornado
A tornado, or twister, is like a small hurricane. The wind spins around a small area of calm in the center. But it spins much faster than a hurricane, moving over the ground at high speed and destroying everything in its path. A tornado spins so fast that it soon loses energy.

Dust Devils
Dust devils are a type of whirlwind that blow in desert areas. They pick up dust as they move over the land.

Jet Stream
The jet stream, high above Earth, is a narrow band of very fast-moving winds.

Rainy Days

In most parts of the world, water falls from clouds in the sky as rain. If it's very cold, it falls as sleet, hail, or snow. Large drops of water fall in heavy showers or thunderstorms. Small waterdrops fall as drizzle. The amount of rain that falls in any place is called its rainfall.

Measuring the Wetness in the Air

The air is **humid**, or damp and moist, when it contains a lot of water vapor. Warm air holds more water vapor than cold air. Damp and humid air is mostly found in the hot, steamy jungles and rain forests near the equator.

Hygrometer

A hygrometer is an instrument that measures how much humidity is in the air. A mechanical hygrometer uses human hair—always blond hair—attached to a dial. The hair expands or contracts depending on the humidity.

Hailstones form in huge storm clouds. They can be as big as tennis balls when they fall, causing a lot of damage.

Dew forms at night when the temperature drops. The droplets **condense** and then fall onto the ground and plants.

The Water Cycle

Water moves from the air to the land and back to the air again and again. This repeated journey is called the water cycle.

2. Rising water vapor changes back into liquid and forms clouds.

3. Water falls as rain or snow.

1. The Sun's energy causes water to evaporate into vapor.

4. Water drains back to sea via rivers.

Cloudburst

A cloudburst is a sudden shower of heavy rain. These often happen in periods of warm and stormy weather.

Hygroscope

A hygroscope is an instrument that shows any changes in humidity. A strip of seaweed is a natural hygroscope because it becomes soft when the weather is humid, and hard and dry when it isn't.

Acid Rain

Acid rain falls from clouds that have become full of chemicals. Acid rain may fall near cities where factories send poisonous fumes, such as sulphur dioxide and nitric acid, into the air. Or these fumes may be carried on the wind far from the factories. Nitric acid forms as the fumes mix with the water in the clouds. This acid rain poisons the soil and rivers. It can kill trees and animals and make people feel sick.

11

Weather Forecasting

We can see what the weather is like today, but how do we know what it will be like tomorrow? We know what to expect through weather forecasting.

The study of our Earth's weather and climate is called **meteorology**. You can watch meteorologists on TV, pointing at a map and telling you where the rain will fall or high winds will blow.

Telling us what kind of weather to expect may look easy, but meteorologists are very skilled scientists. They have to watch what is happening around the world.

Meteorologists measure winds, temperatures, and atmospheric pressure to predict how the weather will change from place to place over the next few days.

Weather Words

Some words a meteorologist must understand:

Weather System— a group of conditions, such as wind, rain, and temperature, that combine to produce a storm or other type of weather.

Front—a sharp change in the temperature of the air. A front happens when a mass of cold air meets a mass of warm air. A cold front is the edge of a cold air mass. A warm front is the edge of a warm air mass.

Meteorologists can tell us if it will be cloudy tomorrow!

Isobar–a line on a weather map that shows places with the same atmospheric pressure. It becomes windy where the lines are close together.

Cyclone–a weather system, similar to a hurricane, with low pressure at its center around which winds are blowing.

Depression–an area of low pressure bringing rain, clouds, and wind.

Weather Stations

Weather stations have been set up around the world to help meteorologists predict the weather and see if it has changed over time. The station shown here contains special instruments to measure the weather.

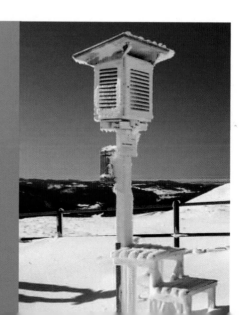

A Cold Day

If you live in a part of the world where your fingers tingle on a cold day, you have probably experienced some of this winter weather!

Hoarfrost (above) is made of ice crystals.

Frost occurs when the air or ground temperature is so cold that ice forms. Moisture in the air, called water vapor, condenses and then freezes on the soil and plants.

Hailstones are the large pieces of ice built of frozen raindrops in a hail storm. Hailstones can be as large as 2 inches (5 centimeters) across.

Sleet is frozen or partly frozen rain. It can be hail that is half melted as it falls.

Snow is water that forms in the clouds as crystals of ice. This can only happen when it is so cold that the water vapor in the clouds freezes.

A **blizzard** is a fierce snowstorm. Blizzards are common in northern areas, especially in icy regions in the Arctic and Antarctica.

Ice is frozen water. Water freezes at 32 degrees Fahrenheit (F) or 0 degrees Celsius. Salty water freezes at a lower temperature, so although the water in a large lake may freeze, seawater usually does not. When water becomes ice, it swells up and takes more space. Even so, ice is lighter and less dense than water, which is why it floats on the water's surface.

Temperature

Fahrenheit is one of the scales used for measuring temperature. On the Fahrenheit scale, water freezes at 32 degrees and boils at 212 degrees.

The other scale is based on the metric system and is called **Celsius**. On the Celsius scale, the freezing point of water is 0 degrees and the boiling point is 100 degrees.

Your average body temperature is 98.6 degrees Fahrenheit (37 degrees Celsius).

A hot day can be 80 degrees Fahrenheit (about 27 degrees Celsius).

A comfortable room temperature is about 70 degrees Fahrenheit (21 degrees Celsius).

Ice Age!

Ice ages are periods of time that can last tens or even hundreds of millions of years. Large areas of the surface of the planet are covered with ice sheets. In between ice ages, there are long times of milder climate called interglacial periods.

Woolly mammoths survived a number of ice ages. Their thick woolly coats probably helped keep them warm!

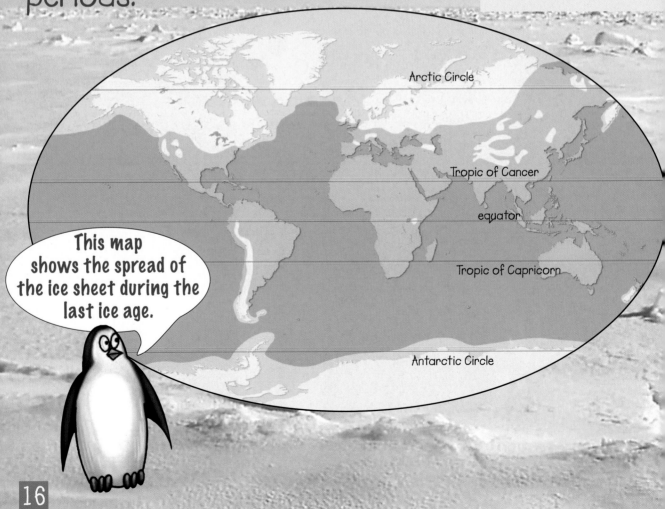

Arctic Circle

Tropic of Cancer

equator

Tropic of Capricorn

Antarctic Circle

This map shows the spread of the ice sheet during the last ice age.

Earth is in an interglacial period now. Although the last ice age ended about 12,000 years ago, we can still see the polar ice sheets and mountain **glaciers** in Alaska, Greenland, and Antarctica that are left over from that time.

Greenhouse Effect

Greenhouses are used to grow plants. The glass panels let in light but keep heat from escaping, so the greenhouse heats up. Gases in the atmosphere trap energy from the Sun in the same way. Without them, heat would escape into space. At night, the temperature would drop to -40 degrees F (-40 degrees C)! These gases are called greenhouse gases. Too much of these gases in the air causes temperature to rise. That is known as global warming.

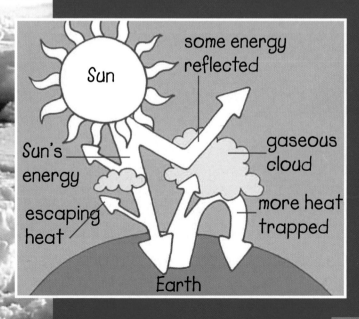

Sun

some energy reflected

Sun's energy

gaseous cloud

escaping heat

more heat trapped

Earth

Clouds

Clouds are made from tiny droplets of water. These droplets are so tiny and light that they can hang in the air without dropping to the ground. When the droplets become heavy enough, they fall as rain, snow, or hail. Clouds can be very high up or close to the ground. The wind shapes them and blows them in different directions.

Cumulonimbus clouds bring stormy weather.

Cloud Shapes

Cirrus–these clouds form very high up in the sky. They look like wispy streaks.

Cirrostratus–these clouds are also high in the sky. They look like a thin veil and usually mean warm weather is coming.

Cirrocumulus–these clouds are made of ice crystals and appear lower in the sky than cirrus clouds. They look like strips with rounded edges.

Altocumulus–these small, rounded clouds form in groups or lines. They sometimes make the Moon or Sun appear to have colored rings.

Altostratus–these clouds form sheets that can sometimes fill the whole sky. They can bring rain or snow.

Cumulus–these are round and fluffy and can be very tall. They often develop in warm weather.

TYPES OF CLOUDS

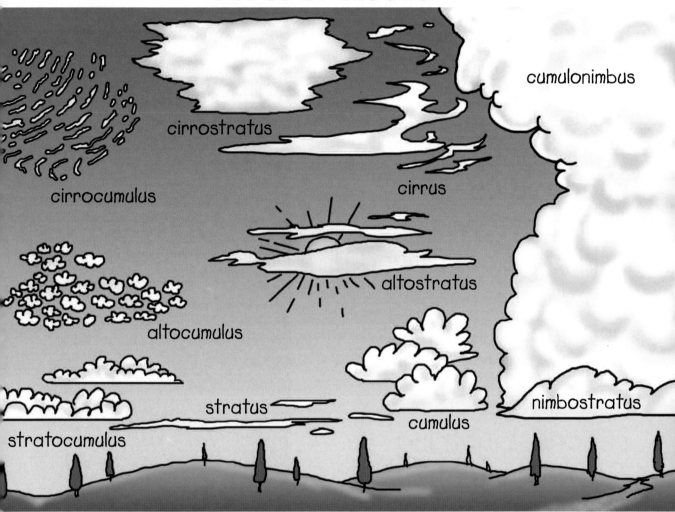

cumulonimbus

cirrostratus

cirrocumulus

cirrus

altostratus

altocumulus

stratus

cumulus

nimbostratus

stratocumulus

Stratocumulus–these clouds can clump together in sheets or have gaps between them. They have dark areas caused by thick rolls of cloud.

Stratus–these are low-lying clouds that form a continuous sheet. They sometimes bring drizzling rain.

Cumulonimbus–these clouds can be huge and dark gray. They bring stormy weather.

Nimbostratus–these clouds usually mean snow. They hang like a dark, gray sheet across the sky.

Bang! Crash!

Thunderstorms can be frightening. Meteorologists tell us that, at any one time, nearly 2,000 thunderstorms are taking place around the world. These produce about 100 lightning strikes that hit Earth each second. Lightning hits chimneys, high buildings, power lines, and radio towers. These objects can be struck more than once during a single storm but aren't always damaged.

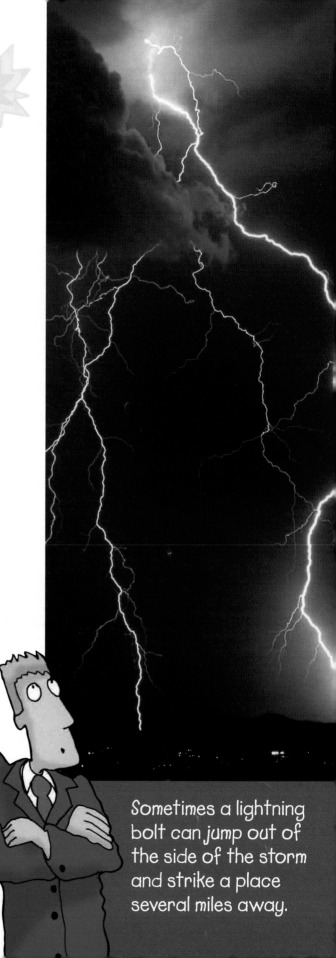

Sometimes a lightning bolt can jump out of the side of the storm and strike a place several miles away.

How Lightning Forms

Thunderstorms happen when strong air currents move high into the sky. This forms huge cumulonimbus clouds that are full of rain. The rising hot air forces cold air to the ground. This movement of air forms strong winds. Powerful "updrafts" and "downdrafts" in the clouds also cause lightning to develop.

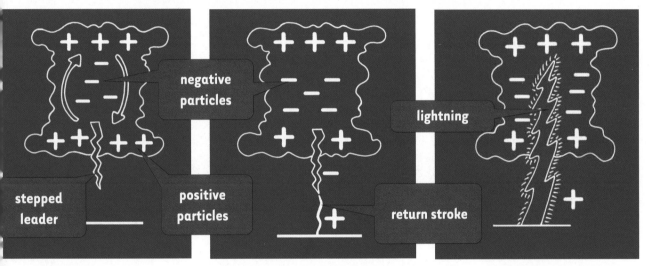

1. The updrafts and downdrafts charge **particles** in the cloud. Positive particles form at the top and bottom of the cloud. Negative particles form in the middle. A thin stroke of negative particles, known as a "stepped leader," heads toward the ground.

2. A positive "return stroke" rises from the ground. This might travel up a tall object, like a telephone pole or chimney.

Did You Know?

The temperature inside a lightning bolt can reach 55,000 degrees F (30,538 degrees C). That's five times hotter than the surface of the Sun!

3. When the two strokes meet, a bright flash of electricity is made. That's what we see as lightning!

The lightning travels up into the cloud, where it quickly heats the surrounding air. This is what causes the thunder crash that we hear moments later.

21

Weather Satellites

Satellites measure changes in the weather from high above Earth. They help meteorologists make more accurate forecasts over a longer period of time.

The Cloudsat satellite is being used to study clouds in ways that had not been possible. Scientists hope to learn more about how clouds affect weather.

This picture of Hurricane Rita (right) was taken from space by the Aqua satellite on September 21, 2005. The "eye" of the hurricane, which the winds swirl around, is clearly visible.

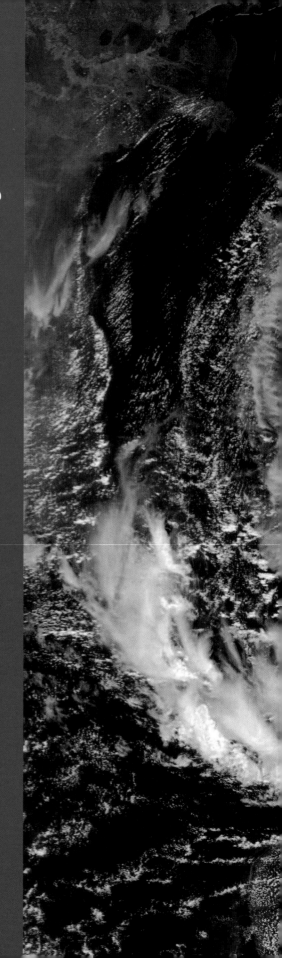

The Lockheed ER-2 is a special plane that flies high above the clouds to study hurricanes. It can fly as high as 69,000 feet (21,030 meters).

eye

Phew! It's Hot!

Heat comes from our Sun, so when it shines directly on our part of the world, we feel warmer. As Earth circles the Sun, different areas tilt toward the Sun, so different parts of the world enjoy lots of sunshine at different times of the year. These sunny months are called summer.

Evaporation

Evaporation describes what happens when a liquid turns into a gas. The Sun heats up water (a liquid) in rivers, lakes, or the ocean and turns it into water vapor (a gas). The water vapor rises into the air as a heat haze. This is a very thin mist. It is caused by warm air rising off the water through the cool air.

The Sun's heat often causes a heat haze over water.

Hot and Dry

A drought is a long period without rain. Plants and animals suffer during a drought. The earth also dries and cracks. Deserts form in places where there are many droughts.

Heat Wave

- While most of us enjoy the summer Sun, high temperatures can be dangerous.
- One of the biggest dangers of a heat wave is dehydration. This means our bodies lose water, including important blood salts like potassium and sodium that help keep our kidneys, brain, and heart working.
- We usually sweat when we get hot. This helps keep us cool. But on very hot days, this system can fail. When that happens, our body temperature can rise.
- The best way to avoid heat problems is to drink water and stay in the shade.

Weather Around the World

A **climatologist** looks at weather over a long time and in specific parts of the world. The climate of a place depends on where it is on the globe—whether it's closer to the equator or the Arctic, for example.

The map on the opposite page shows six different kinds of weather around the world. Can you find each one by matching the colors to the picture keys and descriptions?

Continental—very cold winters, mild summers.

Temperate—mild or cold winters, warm or hot summers. No dry season.

Tropical—hot all year. Some regions have a rainy season and a dry season.

Dry—can be very hot or cold but very little rain all year. Examples are deserts and grasslands.

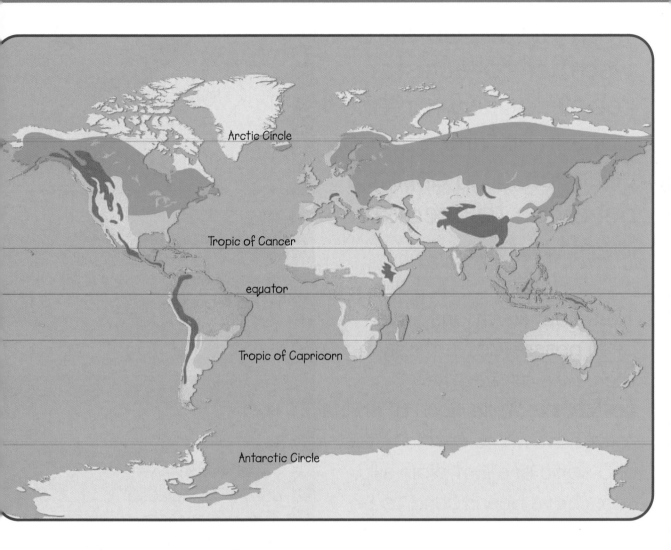

Arctic Circle

Tropic of Cancer

equator

Tropic of Capricorn

Antarctic Circle

Polar–very cold and dry. Covered by ice sheets most of the year. Very short summer.

Mountainous–climate affected by the altitude. High peaks are very cold.

Folklore

What did we do before weather forecasts? People looked for tiny signs in nature, such as changes in an animal's behavior, to predict local weather.

These observations have been passed down through the years as weather **folklore**. While many of these tales have no scientific basis and some are just plain silly, some have been found to be surprisingly accurate. Here are a few!

1. During good weather, the kinds of insects swallows eat are carried up on warm currents rising from the ground.

2. "Seabirds, stay out from the land. We won't have good weather while you're on the sand." Seabirds seem to detect the shifts in air pressure that will bring bad weather.

3. Bees return to their hives and are unlikely to swarm before a storm. They are probably detecting tiny changes in air pressure.

4. Fishermen say that fish "bite" more before a rainstorm, as do small flies. Maybe that's because it's their last chance to feed before the rain.

5. If cows are lying down, you can expect rain.

6. Here's a good one! If you keep making faces, one day the wind will change and you'll get stuck that way!

7. "Red sky at night, sailors' delight. Red sky in the morning, sailors take warning."

8. In Australia, they say: "When the kookaburras call, the rain will fall."

9. If there's a ring around the Moon, it will rain in as many days as there are stars in that ring.

Weather Quiz

Here's a quick weather quiz! Get a piece of paper and a pen, write your answers down, and check them with the answer key below.

1. What type of weather does low pressure air usually bring?

2. What form of weather does the Beaufort scale measure?

3. What is used in a mechanical hygrometer to measure humidity?

4. What does it mean when the isobar lines are close together on a weather map?

5. At 0 degrees Celsisus (32 degrees Fahrenheit), what happens to water?

6. What are interglacial periods?

7. Cirrocumulus and cumulonimbus are examples of what feature of the weather?

8. About how often does lightning strike the ground each second?

9. What happens to a liquid when it evaporates?

10. According to weather folklore, what do cows seem to be expecting when they lie down in their field?

1. Wet 2. Wind 3. A (blond) human hair 4. It's going to be windy! 5. It freezes. 6. Periods between ice ages 7. Clouds 8. 100 9. It becomes a gas. 10. Rain

Glossary

anemometer: an instrument that measures wind speed

atmospheric pressure: also air pressure; the measurement of the weight of air pushing down on an area of the ground

barometer: an instrument used for measuring air pressure

climatologist: a scientist who studies weather patterns, usually over periods of time and in different parts of the planet

condense: to cause a gas, such as water vapor, to turn into a liquid by cooling it down

drought: a period of dryness that can cause a serious drop in the water supply and damage to crops

equator: an imaginary line that circles Earth halfway between the North and South poles

folklore: a set of beliefs and tales that are passed on over the years. Some have bits of truth in them. Some do not.

glaciers: huge moving masses of ice formed by compacted snow, usually over many years

humidity: the amount of moisture, or wetness, in the air

meteorology: the science of studying weather and forecasting weather patterns, usually for periods of a few days or more

particle: a very small or basic bit of matter. When lightning forms, particles in the clouds become electrically charged.

Index